But God...

The Story of My Life

JO ANN CARTY

ISBN: 979-8-88945-455-7

eISBN: 979-8-88945-456-4

Brilliant Books Literary

137 Forest Park Lane Thomasville

North Carolina 27360 USA

Printed in the United States of America

Preface

My name given to me at birth is Jo Ann Jonas. My parents were Ruth and Austin Jonas. They are both now deceased. I am an avid Oprah fan. I can remember her stating in one of her shows that we each have a story to tell. What propelled me to write my story is the message my Pastor, Rico Sharp, preached. The title of his message was, "But God". He too stated that if we could only tell of our experiences and how we survived because of God, we could help someone else. He even went on to say we should use the title, "But God".

I am presently attending Calvary Christian Center with Pastors Dawn and Jim Raley. I recently attended a conference where T.D. Jakes was invited to speak. Because I paid to attend the conference, I had a seat very close to the front. In his message, he looked and pointed in my direction and said, "Write that book". I received the Word from God and decided to complete what I have already written.

I wrote most of my story several years ago at the time Pastor Rico preached his message, but have not had the courage to let someone read it or publish it. I decided to let my brother read it and he loved it. He also said to me that he learned in an Alcohol Anonymous class that you are only as sick as your secrets. I do not like to keep secrets. I am looking forward to the rest of my life with the new husband God will bring to me. I want to be free, honest, an above board. I am looking forward to a peaceful loving relationship.

I wrote my story to be able to help other women who may be struggling with the very situations I've been through. I want to wake them up, so they too can escape the lives they chose and allow God to give them a better life.

My Beginnings

I can remember growing up in the Lincoln Projects in Harlem in New York City. My mother was a diabetic and remained at home. My father worked as a longshoreman on the docks in Brooklyn, New York. I was the middle child. My sister, who had a different father, is fifteen months older than I; my brother, with whom I share the same father, is three years younger. My parents belonged to a holiness church. I went to church on Tuesday evening for Bible study, Thursday evening for missionary service, Friday evening for youth service, and all day Sunday for Sunday school at 10:00 a.m., morning worship at 11:00 a.m., and Sunday evening service at 7:00 p.m. I believed that everything was a sin. I was not allowed to wear pants, makeup, or jewelry. When I turned eleven years old, my mother looked at me in my short pants and said, "You are getting to big to be wearing pants." That was the last time I wore pants, until I became an adult and left home.

School Days

I can remember my first day in Kindergarten. My teacher's name was Mrs. Stevens. I was five years old and had never been separated from my mother. Kindergarten was only for half a day. The first day, I cried incessantly and refused to associate with the other students. Mrs. Stevens gave me a lollipop and said I could spend the day with her. After several days, I soon became acclimated and interacted with the other students. Mrs. Stevens discovered that I knew how to read. I was placed in a first grade classroom. I enjoyed my time with the other first graders. Even though I spent many months of my Kindergarten period in a first grade class, I still was promoted and had to spend another year in the first grade.

During my second grade year, my teacher and I got into an altercation. She was Caucasian and often not very kind to me. I can only remember my mother writing a letter and gave it to me in a sealed envelope to give to my teacher. After reading the note my mother wrote, my teacher was furious and sent me to the principal's office. I saw the assistant principal; she asked me which first grade class I would like to be in. I responded, "I am in the second grade and would like to remain in my class." The assistant principal granted my desire and said I was not to ever bring in a note like that again. Until this day, I have no knowledge of what was written in that note. I know my mom made comments that my teacher often came to work drunk. I was just happy not to be put back into a grade I already passed.

When I was in the fifth grade, I was placed in a special class along with several other students who were very bright. I can remember my teacher's face, her name was Mrs. Richardson. She was very stern. She always used to say, "If something is worth doing, it's worth doing well." This saying has resonated within me, I often find myself saying the same thing.

I went to an all girls junior high school. I joined the glee club. I can remember one of the participants in our group being thrown off the stage during a performance. I don't remember what Penny did, but I can remember the director, Mr. Scott, yelling at her, "Get off, get off now!" I thought it was pretty embarrassing.

I attended Julia Richmond High School my ninth grade year. My music teacher believed I had a nice voice and encouraged me to try out for the High School of Music and Art. She taught me an Italian song, *Caro Mio Bien*. I was accepted and spent the next three years in Music and Art High School. I was told that Diahann Carroll was the first African American to attend this school. This was the first time I made a white friend. Her name is Frances. She even spent the night at my home. My family and I were then living in the Polo Grounds. This was a new project at the time. I saw Willie Mays in person when he came for the dedication of the new buildings. Frances' parents even visited our church when my mom invited them. That was the first time we had white folks in our church. I visited her home in Riverdale. It was like a project building, but the apartment was much larger than mine.

Boyfriends

My very first boyfriend was Jack. He had two sisters who were friends with my sister and me. Their names were Connie and Ramona. We played together everyday. One time my sister and I went to their apartment and were playing music. Jack and I began to dance. His mother peered into the room and I stopped. She smiled and said, "Go ahead." I was fearful because dancing was a sin. My mother used to tell us, "If you kiss a boy you could get pregnant." One time Jack's lips touched mine and I was scared to death. I thought for sure I was going to have a baby. Jack, Connie and Ramona moved away while I was still in elementary school. They came back to visit once, but then I never saw them again. I was fifteen years old when I met Julian. Julian was twenty-four years old. My older sister was light-skinned and was always told by others how pretty she was. No one ever told me I was pretty. My mother did tell me I had pretty eyes. My mother allowed Julian to date me. My mother knew his aunt Maggie very well. They belonged to the same church. My mother told me I was in love with him since I talked about him all the time. My mother was a diabetic and wanted to make certain I was taken care of before she died. We dated, and I was engaged at the age of seventeen. During my senior year of high school, one of the boys walked up to me while I was going to my next class, and gave me a Valentine's card. My friend April was with me at the time. Now I was engaged to Julian and did not know what to do. April quickly took the card and gave it to me and said, "Take it." I later explained to the young man (I forget his name), that I was engaged. Soon after that I saw him with another girl. He got over me very quickly.

The Honeymoon

I got married the summer after graduating high school. We left for the honeymoon the day after the wedding. We did nothing on our wedding night. We waited until we got to the Bahamas. When I returned home and went to church, one of sisters in the church asked me, "How was the honeymoon?" I replied, "It was great!" There was no need of anyone knowing the truth. It hurt and I did not enjoy lovemaking at all. I did not bleed, and Julian accused me of not being a virgin. This was the beginning of twenty-eight years of hell. My mother died before I had any of my children. She came to me in a dream when I had Jonelle. I let her hold Jonelle; then, said to her, "You have to give her back." My mother said she knew to give her back. I felt badly afterwards telling her she have to give her back.

Married Life

I felt like a child who got married. I did not know what to do with myself. When Julian went to work, I went to my mother's. I was there everyday. My father finally said, "You are a married woman and need to be at home." I went to a manpower program and learned how to be a bank teller. I worked for the Chase Manhattan Bank. I went to school to study accounting and ended up with a Bachelor of Business Administration degree with a major in management. I was a teller the whole time I attended college; I barely graduated with a 2.0. Now what was I going to do with my degree? I decided to have children. Julian knelt down to pray just before Jonelle was conceived. During my pregnancy, I had a cyst the size of a grapefruit. It was painful. I could not have it removed because the anesthesia would kill Jonelle in my womb. I went through the healing line at church. When I returned to the doctor he could not locate the cyst at all. God had healed me.

When Jonelle was a year old, I went to work as an accounting clerk. I worked for a year before I conceived another child. After seven weeks, I began bleeding. I was on the job at the time and confided in my older friend, Maxine. Maxine told me to get permission from the supervisor to go to the clinic. She told me my supervisor did not have to know why. I went to the doctor that day and they scraped the baby out of my womb. It was the same as having an abortion. I wept. I thought I would be unable to have more children. Months later, I got pregnant again. I was so very sick during this pregnancy. I told my husband, I was not well. He did not believe me, or he did not care. I tried to take care of Jonelle with much difficulty that day. I told Julian he had to take her to our baby sitter the next day because I could not care for her. I went to the doctor, but the doctor could not prescribe anything because I was pregnant. My friends and the church members came by with food and quickly left. They were afraid to come in the room where I was because they did not know what was wrong with me. They left soup and juices. My best friend, Arnette brought me Tropicana Orange Juice. I can remember that the orange juice she brought me was the only thing that provided taste in my mouth. The soup tasted like dirt. I believed that I was going to die. I stopped watching television and said my prayers and closed my eyes and waited for the death angel. He never came. I had Justin weeks after he was due. His skin was dried up. Justin was my smallest baby. He weighed four pounds and two ounces. He was so tiny he fit in the palm of my husband's hand. My mother had three children, so I decided to go ahead and get pregnant again. I did not want to wait another two years. A lady in the church said to me, "I bet you can't produce another good-looking son like Justin." I am always up for a dare. I got pregnant again and she had to admit I had another good-looking son, Joel. Justin and Joel are fifteen months apart.

My Move To Florida

We lived in Coop City in the Bronx when we had our children. Julian and I wanted to purchase a house, so we went to Florida for a visit. My mother had a first cousin who lived in Central Florida and we stayed with him and his family. They loaned us their car and Julian and I and the children went to Disney World for the first time. Joel was a baby, Justin was about two and Jonelle was four. When we arrived at Disney World, the first trip was to the restroom. I had to change Justin and Joel's diapers and then get everyone something to drink. I decided the next time we go to Disney the children will be old enough to use the restrooms by themselves.

We looked at the different homes for sale in Central Florida. We decided to purchase a home in Lake Mary. We moved to Lake Mary the very next year. We sold all of our furniture and Julian loaded up the car and sent me and the children by plane to Florida. There was a snow storm in New York at the time. My plane could not leave because of the storm. That night the children and I had to make a bed on the floor. My dad and his wife lived in another section of Coop City. They told me to come over and stay until my flight could leave. A brother in the church drove us to the airport the next day. The brother was late. The plane was leaving at 2:00 p.m. and he comes to pick us up in a school bus. It was 2:00 p.m. and we were still on the road. I knew we would never make it. David said, "Just have faith." I had none. When we arrived at the airport, my plane was still there. I was shocked. David said, "I told you to have faith." My faith certainly increased that day.

Life in Florida

We looked through the phone book to find our church, The Church of God of Prophecy. The Church of God of Prophecy has local churches in every state in the United States and on many of the Caribbean Islands, and many countries throughout the world. The headquarters for the church is in Cleveland, Tennessee. We found an address in Sanford, Florida, which was not far away. We arrived for Sunday school. We did not see any black people in the class. I thought perhaps they are in a different class. When we assembled for church, I looked around at the entire congregation. We were the only black people in the entire congregation. After church we spoke with the pastor and asked where did the black people attend? They said that the black people attended a church not far from the location where we were. The pastor did not want to give us the address because he wanted us to continue to come to his church. His wife said they prayed for a black family to come to their church and here we are. We did visit the black Church of God of Prophecy. They had a curtain in front of the stall in the bathroom. I had to walk through the mud to get to the church building. What church do you think we decided to join? We were an answer to prayers, so we were the first black people to join the Elm Avenue, Church of God of Prophecy.

The pastor's wife was a school teacher in a nearby church and said they needed another teacher. She knew I had a bachelor's degree and recommended me to be the teacher. I finished out the last two months of the school-year and worked the entire year the next school-year. I decided to go back to school to get my certification to teach mathematics. Julian was not happy with this. He insisted that I have another child. The devil is a liar. My father told me Julian wanted me to be barefoot and pregnant. I substituted in the public school system and used the money to pay for my education. When I received my certification I decided to continue my education. I knocked on every door at the University of Central Florida inquiring about a scholarship. I finally did receive the Delores Auzenne Scholarship for ten thousand dollars. This allowed me to obtain my masters degree in Educational Leadership.

My husband of course was not very happy. Every other year since we got married, he would take me to his home in the Virgin Islands. When I got the children, he used to make the trip alone. My children and I were happy when Julian would leave us. One Sunday, he called and asked if we were getting ready for church. I said we are getting ready but not for church. I took some money out of the bank and the children and I went to Universal Studios. Justin and Joel, who used to always fight, did not fight this day. We all had a wonderful time. The children at the time were about 8, 9 and 12 years old. Life was miserable when Julian was at home. He would turn off the air-conditioner at night. He would buy old bread at the thrift store. When you took a slice out of the package, the bread would break. Every time I received my paycheck, I had to give it to him. He believed I did not know what to do with the money. I believed, though, he would always take care of me. I soon learned this was not true.

The Divorce

I used to complain to any one who would listen how miserable I was in my marriage. My cousin used to tell me to stop paying the mortgage. She said Julian would never let the house get away from him. In addition to the school-year, I used to work every summer and handed over my paycheck to him. I thought he was putting up money for the both of us. I remember he asked me to sign some papers. I trusted him so much; I did not even read the papers. I soon learned he had a significant amount of money in his IRA and I had a much lower amount. My church did not believe in divorce and remarriage. That is why I stayed for twenty-eight years. I tried many times to make it work. I wanted us to have prayer as a family. We would always get into an argument and not pray. There were wires sticking me from the bed. I told Julian we needed a new mattress; he refused to buy one. I bought a mattress with my own money. Julian got heavier during our marriage and his snoring was outrageous. He even hit me once while he was sleeping. My friend asked, "Are you sure he didn't hit you on purpose?" I then began to sleep on the couch. One time Julian and I argued in the kitchen. Julian hit me so hard on my hand it stung me for at least two days. Of course at the time, I did not believe that this was abusive. I saw it as a one time act of anger. I am an Oprah fan. I saw her show since it first came on. She said if he hit you once he will do it again. Oprah was right. I was in the bedroom with my daughter; my husband and I were having another one of our arguments. He picked up an iron to hit me. I grabbed the phone to call the police. He pulled the plug out of the wall, put the iron down, and fled the house fearing the policeman. The police never showed. Julian must have pulled the plug before the 911 number connected. I knew I had to leave this marriage. I left and moved into a nearby apartment when my boys were still in elementary school and my daughter was in middle school. I only had an assistant teaching job at the time and expected my husband to pay alimony. He convinced me he would change and spoke with the landlord. They let me out of my lease. Of course my relationship with Julian had gotten worse. We no longer had sexual relations. I slept on the couch. I felt like I was living with a stranger. He tried to rape me once. I laid still. When I was able to, I got up ran to the bathroom and locked the door. I never mentioned this to anyone. I discussed with my best friend about leaving Julian. I felt dead in my spirit. I believed if I stayed with Julian, I would still go to hell because I had no joy. My friend convinced me I would make it this time. I had a full-time teaching position. I had a master's degree. My daughter was in college; Justin and Joel were in high school. I told Julian I was leaving. He smiled. He even helped me to load the truck. I suppose he wanted to get rid of me too.

Life without Julian

I moved into a three bedroom apartment since Jonelle was away at college. Justin and Joel still did not get along well, so they each needed their own room. I had purchased my own car during the marriage at the advice of one of my cousins. Life was peaceable for the most part until my last son, Joel began giving me trouble. Both Justin and Joel at this time were six-feet tall. Joel was very angry and very disrespectful. He was always getting into trouble at school. One day I decided to take the day off and arrange to shadow Joel in school for the day. I secretly made the arrangements with one of Joel's assistant principals. To my surprise, Joel was happy to see me. He held my hand when we traveled from one class to the next. During lunch he left me with his brother to eat. During lunch Joel played ball with his friends. He came back for me and even kissed me on the cheek. His friends remarked, "No wonder you are behaving today, your mom is here." I had a pleasant day with Joel in his high school. Joel wanted me to come again. Joel's behavior did not change. He was suspended numerous times. One time his sister had a car accident and I had to leave school immediately to prepare to travel to North Carolina to see about Jonelle. Joel of course was suspended again that day. I stopped at the high school to pick him up and he helped me pack and I left for the airport. Julian did not offer to give me one dime. It was an unexpected trip and Jonelle needed her parents. Even before I left Julian, I was mother and father to my children. Julian never attended any function the children were in. Justin was captain of the freshmen football team. Julian refused to pay the $6.00 to see his son play. Jonelle was happy to see me. The car was totaled. Her best friend who was in the car at the time of the accident was suing her. I called the young lady's parents to let them know how sorry I was their daughter was in the accident. I also told them neither Jonelle nor I had any money for them to sue. They did not sue, and Jonelle and her friend made up and continued their friendship.

Jonelle soon graduated from college and came home to live. She wanted to have her own apartment, but soon learned of life's expenses and decided to live with her brothers and me instead. Jonelle was very persuasive. She would say, Mom, let's see how much it cost to have a gym membership; I would stop and inquire and soon Jonelle and I had a membership at the gym. Jonelle decided to continue her education at Stetson University while living at home. Her professor gave her students the option of taking a trip to Europe in lieu of the class and the students would receive credit for having taken the class. The trip cost more than $4,000 per person. Jonelle said, "Mommy we could do this." I gave in and used the refund from my tax return to pay for my trip. Jonelle worked and with my help was able to pay for her own trip. There were fourteen of us altogether who went on the trip. Our first stop was Paris, France. I said, "Jonelle, pinch me; I can't believe I'm in Paris." We visited Amsterdam, Holland, St. Petersburg, Russia, and Denmark. I know if I stayed with Julian, I would have never made this trip. Later that year, I felt harassed by my administrator at school. He was saying the parents were complaining about me and would not give me the names of the parents. I knew what students were giving me trouble and I decided to call their parents. After dialoging with the parents, I insisted they speak to my supervisor to assure him the matter was settled. Sure enough my administrator had to give me a good evaluation because there was nothing negative he could say about me. Again, I began to feel harassed the next school-year. I decided to go to the county office to speak with the superintendent for the middle schools. I had intended to let him know what was happening to me at the middle school. I had been in this particular school now for at least eight years. The superintendent was not in his office. His assistant was annoyed that I was there to complain about the principal. She proceeded to tell me what a good man my principal was. I did not mention I was going to complain about the principal. I just wanted to let the Superintendent know what I was feeling and wanted to get his suggestion for keeping my job. Soon after that conversation with the superintendent's assistant, I was harassed even more. A new assistant principal was hired, and she was out to get me. One of my co-workers left the school to work at an alternative school because she did not like what was going on at the school. Every class was required to have reading as a portion of the grades. My co-worker taught science and was not happy to add reading as a portion of the grade. If a student read well, he/she would enhance all of his/her grades by 10%. If the student chose not to read, he or she would have a reduction of 10% of his/her grade in every subject. All the teachers were not allowed to give input. This was decided by the administration and maybe certain teachers. My co-worker told me they need people where she was. I applied and was hired. Instead of a teaching job, I was placed as a supervisor because of my certification in Educational Leadership. I was happy to leave the school system and even made more money. My tenure as an administrator was short-lived. After the Florida Comprehensive Assessment Test (FCAT) was given in February, all of the administrators lost their position. Some left to find other jobs. I was placed back in the classroom. I decided to go back to the public school system since I had to teach. I accepted a position in the middle school where my children had attended. The white parents did not want me there. I thought since I was hired by a black assistant principal I was safe. I had made a wrong assumption. She evaluated me and said she had no problems with me. The mathematics coordinator for the district came to my classroom and said, "Your children love you." After giving the students the grades they deserved on the first progress report, I was called into the principal's office and was asked to resign. When I came home, my daughter said, "Mommy, you do not have a job?" I said to my children we are going to worship God. My older son Justin had a job as a dishwasher at the time. When he received his pay he brought every penny to me. I never had to ask. I will never forget the love and compassion, and selflessness my son exhibited.

Later that year my aunt was telling me she was going on a cruise. My aunt had already been on several cruises during her lifetime. Her husband was a custom officer on the ships in the Virgin Islands and she lived an extraordinary life. My daughter said to me, "Mommy, let's see how much it cost to go on a cruise." Again, I listened to her and she and I and her brothers went on our first cruise that December. I still had not gotten another job. When my aunt was telling me of her cruise, she was speaking of her death. While we were on the cruise, my aunt died. The cruise was my best vacation ever. I loved dressing for dinner each evening. My daughter coerced me into going snorkeling. When I was told the water was twenty feet deep I refused to go. A lady decided I could stay with her. I took her arm and as we headed for the water, she soon left me. I decided to stay on shore. One of the workers from the island came to get me. He promised he would not leave me. He gave me an inflatable inner tube. He, Jonelle, and I proceeded into the water. I hung on to the inner tube with all my might. The worker left us to go down into the water to get a conch shell. I would have drowned if my daughter hadn't yell at me, Calm down and stop grabbing the inner tube". I held it lightly and found that I began to float. I soon got the hang of putting my face in the water and breathing through the snorkel. It was wonderful to see the world under the sea. I saw a school of fish. I could not believe I was dangling and looking under the water at twenty feet above the ground. God is certainly good. During the evenings aboard ship, I went to the early show. I usually went to bed by 10:00 p.m. while my children wandered the ship and partied until late in the evening. One night I went dancing all alone. I did the *Electric Slide*. As an adult, I learned that dancing was not really a sin and it was all right to wear pants. My daughter had me looking like a younger woman by working out at the gym and changing my eating habits. One man was surprised to learn that I was the mother of my children; he did not believe I was old enough to have adult children. I was looking good; thank God. Our seven days of cruising was coming to an end. The last port was Nassau in the Bahamas. When I arrived, I borrowed a cell phone from one of the natives to call my cousin to come and get us. While waiting, I saw two of my other cousins who were downtown for various reasons. My children got a tour of the island. They had never had the opportunity before this to visit the Caribbean Islands. My cousin drove us to visit my mother's brother and her last sister. My uncle had gotten very old and did not know me. I had a conversation with my aunt and gave her some money, introduced her to my children, prayed with her and left. When I got home and told her older sister who live here in Florida that I had been to Aunt Lela's house, she said to me, "Lela called her and said, "Someone was here and gave me some money and introduced me to her children, but I don't know who she is." My aunt said, "Well you could have asked her who she was." My aunt in Florida explained to her sister in Nassau who I was. When I was about 12 years old when I spent a whole summer in Nassau with this aunt who now does not even know who I am. My cousin took us to get some cracked conch. It is like fish and chips with conch substituting for the fish. We were happy they allowed us to bring it with us on board the ship. It was delicious. The next day we were headed home. We hated for the cruise to end. I still was in need of a job.

My Life in Georgia

I decided since I could not get a job in Florida, I would try Georgia. I had an interview in Cobb County. I had a cousin who lived in Marietta and went to stay with her. Her daughter picked me up from the airport and drove her car like a maniac on the highway. I was in the back seat praying to God to let me live. We arrived at her apartment in the morning. I decided to take a nap. My cousin was not going to be home until 7:00 o'clock that evening. My cousin's daughter and her first cousin sat and talked. I talked with them. They got hungry and ate cold cereal. No one offered me anything. Did they not know I was hungry too? I said nothing. When my cousin arrived at 7:00 p.m., she began to cook while we talked about old times. Her son and his girlfriend came over to eat. When I looked for my share, my cousin said the food was not yet ready. It was ready enough for her son to be eating. I went in the room and called my former pastor on the phone and asked if I could stay with them. He told me to have my cousin drive me to his home. His home was about an hour away. I told my cousin, I would be staying with the pastor. It was about 10:00 p.m. when I decided to leave. I told her daughter to please stop some place where I could get something to eat. We went to a chicken place and I got some chicken and fries. Her daughter was driving at 80 miles per hour and putting in a CD at the same time. She was blasting the music. Again I was praying to God, while in the back seat of the car, to let me live. When we arrived at my former pastor's home, he came outside to meet me. My cousin was floored when she saw the home; I was too. It was a million-dollar home. I quickly gave my cousin some money, got out of the car, and thanked God for the home I was about to spend the night in. I got lost initially, but soon learned my way around the three story million-dollar home. I stayed on the top floor with my own bathroom of course. God is surely good!!

My pastor took me to the interview the next day. Every one was very nice to me. The human resource director said she picked my resume out of five hundred others because I know how to write. She stated she got resumes from people with doctorate degrees who could not even write a decent sentence. She told me, she would help me find a teaching position and then would help me to move to up to an administrative position. I believed her. When I returned home to Florida, I emailed the woman; she never responded. I suppose I was not the right color. I soon received another invitation to another school district in Georgia. This time I took my daughter with me. We drove to my former pastor's house. I was well rested and with both my daughter and I taking turns driving, the seven-hour trip did not seem long. When we arrived, no one was home. My daughter was so excited. She walked around the outside of the house taking pictures. My pastor and his wife soon arrived and we were able to go inside. There was a gospel concert that weekend. People came from several states to attend the concert. I met two of my cousins from the Bahamas who had come with the choir from the Bahamas. They sang beautifully. I interviewed with Dekalb County earlier that day and was offered the position. My daughter got permission from Stetson University to complete her internship as a guidance counselor in one of Dekalb County's School. My daughter, my older son and I moved to Georgia. Joel chose to stay in Florida. I cleaned my house and put it up for sale. Joel eventually, after staying with friends, moved into his father's home with his father and father's wife and her children.

Before leaving Georgia, I purchased a brand new car. A Toyota Camry was my dream car and I purchased it. I should have had someone with me to purchase the car. I knew absolutely nothing. They told me my monthly payments and did not bother to tell me how much the car cost. I decided the rate was too much and told my daughter, "Let's go." I should have quickly driven off. Another man came out and persuaded me to come back in and coaxed me into buying the car. I knew I needed a car and proceeded to sign the paperwork. I left my vehicle, a 2000 Chevrolet, which was already paid for with Joel. I thought he would get a job and use the car to transport himself. I ended up paying $5,000 more than the car is worth. I left the car with my former pastor and retrieved it when I moved. Joel ended up totaling the car I gave him because his father put a cheap tire on it. The tire burst while Joel was driving from a friend late one evening. His father was right there in Florida, but guess who Joel called when he got into the accident, me. I told him to ask the police officer to drive him home.

My job at the high school was going well in Dekalb County. I was hired as a Title 1 mathematics teacher. I was not to have more than fifteen students in my class. I was also given an assistant teacher. As more and more students entered the school, my class size grew. My assistant teacher was taken away from me and I was no longer a Title 1 teacher. The students were very challenging. One of the other mathematics teachers was hit in the head with the door to her classroom by a student. She quit. Each of us was asked to take one of her classes and we would receive an increase in pay. It sounded good at the time, but I soon learned we forfeited a plan period for an additional $15.00 in our paychecks. I was so angry, but I agreed to do it and had to suffer the extra duty. Dekalb tested their mathematics students every three weeks. The teachers were laden with giving and grading these tests, making a failure list, and calling the home of each student on the list. Remember, I did not have a plan period, and I was still expected to get these reports done and completed in a timely fashion. During the month of October, I had a fire in my home. My daughter did not want the soup I made for dinner and decided she would fry something. She put the oil on the stove and told her brother to watch it. I was working at the computer in my pajamas. When I turned around, my kitchen was on fire. My daughter was still in the bedroom. My son and I ran to the kitchen trying to put the fire out. I was looking in my cabinet for flour. My son had taken a cloth and put over the fire on the stove. He then took the cloth and threw it on the floor. The cloth hit my right foot. I left the apartment screaming. I looked at my foot and saw the skin peel backward. My daughter had escaped on the terrace of our apartment. The fire truck came and the firemen put out the fire and had a big fan to get rid of the smoke. I sat on top of a car with my pajamas on. They call the paramedics and I was taken to the hospital across the street. My daughter did not know I was hurt until we met outside. Both she and her brother began blaming each other. I stopped them and told them it was an accident. I called my supervisor while I was in the hospital. I was home in bed for three weeks. I was in severe pain. I usually do not take drugs, but I lived on pain killers for those three weeks. I ran out of pills and asked my son who had just gotten his driver's license to go to the clinic down the street to get me a refill for my pain pills. His sister was interning at the time and was not home. He was afraid to drive and was giving me excuses not to go. I know what a drug addict felt when he/she did not get the drug. I was in pain and needed the pills. I called my brother in New York and after he finished talking with his nephew, Justin went to get my pills. My principal called me after several days. I told her how much pain I was in. She stated there are drugs for that. I had not started the medication yet when she had called. After two weeks I received a threatening letter from the county stating I would lose my job if I did not return to work. I could not believe the letter. I was being seen at the burn clinic in Atlanta and received a note to take to my job. The pain had subsided and I was able to drive myself to work. So, to avoid losing my job, I went to work even though the wound had not healed. I attended the math department meeting and was reprimanded by the mathematics coach for not thanking the teachers in the mathematics department for filling in for me when I was not there. In the next faculty meeting, I got up and thanked the teachers and the mathematics coach for taking my classes in my absence. When I told them about the fire, everyone seemed shocked. I was told by many teachers that they did not know. The principal and the assistant principal who knew did not bother to inform my colleagues. The next day at work, I received a basket of fruit from the hospitality committee with an apology. The principal and her assistant prepared a professional development plan for me. The principal set me up with a class full of behavior problems. She came in evaluated me and gave me a needs improvement. Later that year to my surprise, another assistant principal came unannounced to evaluate me. I received an excellent evaluation, but was still dismissed at the end of the school-year. I was told I could not ever work in Dekalb County Schools again. I wrote the superintendent a letter while at the school. He was in the building the next day, but he only spoke with the principal. I was not treated fairly, but I had no advocate. Again, I had to search for a job.

My Quest To be Married

When my ex remarried two years after I left him, my dad called me and told me, "You don't have a husband, so if you want one go and get one." My god-father who is a minister in the church I grew up in told me the same thing. I was surprised. I decided, after about eight years, that I wanted a relationship that will eventually lead to marriage. By the way, we found out my ex was getting married when my son, Joel went to school one day and was told by the pastor's son that they were going to be related because Joel's dad was marrying his aunt. This pastor who pastors one of The Church of God of Prophecy churches that I grew up in counseled my ex and I; then, he performed the marriage of my ex to his sister-in-law. It was years before I learned this. I registered with E-Harmony. It was an experience. I liked people who did not like me and vice-versa. One man invited me to his home in New Orleans and I went. I trusted him. He had pictures of himself with President Bush (the son). I had a great time in New Orleans. He took me to a luncheon with a lot of important people. I attended a party for a candidate who won his election and I attended the State Fair. I saw Stevie Wonder and was able to listen to a concert given by Paul S. Morton and his choir. I had a great time. The gentleman called me to make certain I arrived safely back in Florida, and then, we never spoke again.

I had a white man interested in me. My daughter always tells me if our Zodiac signs do not match, then do not get involved. The white man is a Pisces and I am a Gemini. We spoke on the phone several times, but I was not feeling him. He wanted to come to see me. My friend suggested if I was not feeling him, I better not have him come for a visit. I wrote him a message on E-harmony stating our hearts are not in the same place. There was a minister insisting that I respond to him. He was fat an unattractive and I refused to write to him. I decided to register with Christian mingle hoping to find the right man. Christian Mingle is different from E-harmony. You can peruse all the men and if the man you peruse likes you he can respond. I perused several. To my surprise, a good-looking man, who I believed to be a doctor and minister responded. I said, "Thank you Jesus." We wrote each other one Friday night when I was online. I gave him my number and he asked if it was too late for him to call. I said, "No." He called and we spoke at length that night. I thought he was in Tennessee because of the address on his profile. I found out he was in Georgia and was only three hours from me. He came to see me later in the week. He called to warn me I may not like what I see. When he arrived he asked if he looked like the guy in the picture. I said, "No." I decided to put away my prejudices and give this guy a try. He was much older looking and not as good-looking as the picture he used on the Christian Mingle website. The profile stated he was 53. He was 60 years old. I allowed him to stay in my home. My bedroom had a separate bath. I stayed in my daughter's room. I took him to a gospel concert I had already paid for. My daughter was supposed to accompany me, but she made other plans. It cost me twenty dollars to park the car. I thought he would offer to pay. We held hands the entire time. I hadn't had a man in a long time. That was my problem. All the signs were there, but I refused to see them. This man stated he wanted to marry me after knowing me four months.

He was living with a former girlfriend and still married to his wife. He suckered me into paying my tithes to a ministry that did not exist. He insisted that he just lost a trucking job. He insisted his former girlfriend was just a friend and he was helping her after her husband died. I even had the pleasure of meeting her. She gave me a strange look. Later I decided to call her to find out what their relationship is. She believes he is going to marry her. They do not sleep together according to her and her house belongs to her. He does not give her anything for it. When he learned we talked, he was angry. He yelled at her and told her to stay out of his business. His business was to find woman and take as much of their money as he could. We parted after I learned an expensive lesson. I chose not to meet anyone else online. I did meet someone at a car dealership when I had my oil changed. I was reading my Bible and he came over to me. He tried to sell me a car. I decided, since I found out he too was a Christian, to tell him about the minister/health doctor. He insisted that I drop him and never call him again. He proceeded to give me his number and asked for mine. He called intermittently for three months before I discovered he wanted a relationship with me. I hadn't even remembered what he looked like. He wanted to come to visit me. He lived in Georgia, and by now I had moved back to Florida. I told him to send me his picture via email. He did. I did not recognize this man. Joel remarked, "He looks like grandpa." He made plans to come see me and then at the last minute cancelled. My father died and I had to go to Texas. I stopped in Georgia, so this man agreed to meet me on my trip home. He was very nice and pleasant. He bought me dinner. He kissed me several times. I was surprised and very uncomfortable because I like to kiss in private, and I would like to make the decision whether or not I wanted to be kissed. The security officer came over to discourage us from kissing. At this point, I was on my way back going through security. He was supposed to come to Florida that weekend. He called to cancel the trip. He insisted his business was preventing him from coming. Now prior to this he was telling me how God gave me to him, and he was anxious to see me. During a phone call he mentioned his former girlfriend. He even stated, "Maybe God wants you to go back to your ex-husband." I suppose he reunited with his former girlfriend and had to get rid of me. I have decided to take a break from men. The pain was too much. You can't even trust someone who says they know Jesus. I have been told by every man in my life, including my ex-husband, that I am beautiful. My ex-husband is trying to get back into my life. He is still married to his wife. I do not ever want to reunite with him. I believe God has a God-fearing man waiting for me and I am preparing myself to meet him. The Bible says, "A man who findeth a wife findeth a good thing" Proverbs 18:22. I am waiting to be found.

Waiting To See What The End is going To Be

I returned to Florida since my home did not sell and prayed for a job. I was hired at a high school in Osceola County. I called and asked the Seminole County Public School Human Resource department if I could return. I was told yes, but I cannot get an interview for any position. I did have one interview in Seminole County for an assistant principal position, but when the principal saw me, he proceeded to conduct the interview knowing he would never hire me. When I returned home the same position was back on the vacancy list. I interviewed and accepted a teaching position in a "D" school in Osceola County. I knew that was trouble, but like I told the assistant principal, "I do have to eat." I taught one hundred seventy-two students for six periods in a school day. The principal conducts the evaluation for all new teachers. She was concerned that I hadn't learned all the names of my students and was not able to identify who was ESE and who was ESOL. She stated, "The next time I come into your room you need to have this information." During the mathematics meeting that week I vented my frustration. I could not retrieve the testing information from a computer program and I could not print the list of my students with their labels. I was yelled at by the mathematics coach. I was told by another teacher her response to me was uncalled for. Later that week the assistant principal came into my room. The next day, Friday, I was escorted by this same assistant principal to the principal's office. The assistant principal told lies on her evaluation of me and the principal announced that I was fired and to please turn in my badge and key. I was surprised and asked, "May I ask why?" The principal replied for the reasons stated. I was fired based on the lies concocted by the assistant principal. She stated my class was chaotic. I only had eighteen students in the class at that time. These students and I had a good rapport. Not wanting to get me in trouble, one of my students feared to express she did not understand. I told her not to be afraid to say she did not understand if she indeed did not understand. I proceeded to re-teach and to have the students repeat in unison the transitive postulate. My students began stating, "Oh now I get it." That is when the assistant principal decided to leave the room. She never mentioned any of this in her evaluation. She stated that I did not call my students by name. I called several students by name in her presence. The principal obviously had already made up her mind to dismiss me. And instead of coming to evaluate me herself as she said she would, sent the assistant principal to do her dirty work for her. I am presently looking for work here in the state of Florida or in the State of Georgia where I am certified and highly qualified. I am a child of God and believe with all my heart that he promised never to leave or forsake me. David said, "I was young and now I'm old, never have I seen the righteous forsaken nor his seed begging bread" Psalm 37:25. I am still waiting for God to give me a job and for God to have my next husband to find me. When that happens, I will be able to continue the saga of my life.

My Life Continues

It was December and I still did not have a job. The church I was attending had a Christmas Banquet planned. I made the decision to go since the pastor reduced the price of the tickets. I got all dressed up, took a picture for ten dollars when I arrived, and proceeded to have a wonderful time at the banquet. I looked in my garage for a picture I had taken when I was in acting school. I decided to write Tyler Perry's people with the hopes of getting any part in his picture. I discovered a book I had purchased and never remember reading. The name of the book was *The Prayer of Jabez*. It was a little book written by Bruce Wilkinson. I could not put the book down. I have been praying the prayer every morning since I started reading the book. I have read the book at least six times and have kept a journal as recommended by the author. The week after Christmas, I received a call from a principal in a high school in Athens, Georgia. She stated she wanted someone to begin when school starts in January. I told her I could come on Tuesday for an interview. She told me not to bother to make two trips. I went on Friday and started work when school began the very next week. I was concerned with taking the car and leaving my older son with no transportation to school and his job at Disney. My younger son had a friend who had lived in Athens, Georgia. I called him and he told me there was a bus system in Athens. He also told me of a place in Athens to live. I took his word and came for the interview and rented the apartment the same day. The county provided me with my own laptop computer. The apartment is furnished and was really made to house the university students. I only pay half the rent and have access to only one of the bedrooms in the apartment. I take the bus to work and feel very blessed that God provided transportation for me, so I could leave my vehicle with my older son. I enjoyed my new job as a mathematics support teacher at one of the high schools in Clarke County. I ate lunch with the other math teachers and one teacher in particular did not eat because he was on a fast. I was not attending a church at the time and decided I too needed to fast. I looked up a pastor's website in Florida and followed the fast he proposed to his church. It was the Daniel fast and he and his members were fasting for 21 days and reading the Book of Acts. I started several days afterward, but was determined to fast. I decided to fast for my children to have a closer relationship to God and for a husband. I shopped for my fasting food. I was not to eat sugar, or any meat. I was used to eating healthy, so this fast was not too tough. I was very specific when I prayed to God for a husband. I asked God for someone who was a Christian and someone who was near my age. I told God, He knows who I am, and I need to be comfortable with his looks. My friend, Aurora insisted I find a church home. My assistant principal told me about her church. She said they provided transportation for anyone who wanted to attend. The buses did not run on Sundays. I called and made arrangements to go to church. I searched my closet and saw a suit I had never worn. The tags were still on it. I just had my hair done the week before. I felt beautiful. When I went to church, I heard the hymns I used to sing in my own church I grew up in. I felt God's presence and decided this would be my church. Of course I looked at the men in the church and quickly decided I will not look, but allow

God to let him find me. By this time I had fasted for two weeks. At the end of the service, the pastor provided an opportunity for anyone to join if they so desired. A young man came forward for membership. He stated he was new to Athens and pointed to a sister in the church who had helped him find his way using the buses. She was a bus driver. He had a beautiful smile. I decided I would welcome him to Athens and let him know I too am new here. After church I saw him, but he was busy talking with others so I left the building to wait for the van. The van was not yet there, so I returned to the church building. This time the young man was alone. We shook hands, and I welcomed him and let him know I too am new to Athens. His first words to me were, "Are you married?" This surprised me. I let him know I was not married. We spoke for a short while and I left again to look for the van. The van was not yet there, so I went to the fellowship hall because the pastor mentioned there would be a chili cook-off. When I entered the door, this young man was there. He said, "I was just coming to get you." He boldly asked me how old I was. I did not respond. Then he proceeded to tell me he was over fifty. He looked much younger. I then told him, I too am over fifty. He thought I was 37 or 40 years old. He asked me for my phone number and called me twice the next day. I decided the next Sunday to invite him to dinner, so we could get to know one another better. We discovered we were both the same age. We were born the same year. My birthday is two months before his. He said he could not get me out of his thoughts. He too was praying for God to bring someone into his life. Teddy confided in me that he did drugs, spent years in prison, and he was a married man. He said he got married because a friend of his got married. He stayed with his wife for about two years and left. He had not been with her for about 22 years. He asked her for a divorce when he was in jail, but she decided he was not in a good place to make that decision. She refused to give him a divorce. He also confided that while in prison, he found out he had a lung disease and was told he would be dead by 2005. We have been together ever since we met. I now know what love at first sight means. Within two weeks of knowing each other, we each declared our love for one another. I made certain he stated his feelings first before I stated mine. God is so good. He gave me someone to complement me and I him. This man has been in my prayers ever since we've met. He told me he immediately told his sister, who is a minister about me. We both believe God brought us together. To God Be the Glory! We plan to be married. His name is Teddy. Again, Teddy called his wife to ask for a divorce. I heard him yelling at her. I decided to write her a letter and let her know of our relationship and ask her to sign the divorce papers and she would not have to pay anything. She called Teddy about three weeks later and consented to signing the divorce papers.

Life in Athens with Teddy

After only a week of getting to know Teddy, he asked me if he could move in. He described his living arrangements. He was in a place called "The Healing Place". This was a place where men with addictions were housed. The living space is vey small and Teddy was not allowed to have many personal items, not even a phone while living there. I did not give it much thought and said yes to his living in my apartment. I had never done anything like this in my entire life. I believed in my heart God brought this man into my life. He had just joined the church, so I believed he wanted to live the life of a Christian, he was near my age and he was good-looking. My close friends and family thought I lost my mind when they learned I was living with a man. Teddy took me to visit his sisters and other family members who lived about two hours away. One of his sisters who is a minister, told me of the addictions that existed in her family. She told me Teddy will take me on the ride of my life. I did not know at the time what she meant. I soon learned. The first time Teddy collected his salary from his new job at the poultry, he disappeared for two days. I did not know where he was and he did not answer his phone. I then, decided he needed to leave my home. He came home and sobbed like a baby begging me to forgive him and insisting he would never do it again. Of course, I forgave him.

This was the first of several disappearances. I made an appointment to get my hair done. I had $3000 in my purse, which I had to purchase a vehicle for myself. I had already purchased a Mercedes Benz thanks to Teddy. We both needed transportation and he had agreed he would make the payments if I made a down-payment. We saw a vehicle for sale and made arrangements to purchase it. That is why I had the $3000 in my purse. When Teddy realized I had the money in my purse, he suggested that I give it to him and he would take it home after dropping me off. I felt a little uncomfortable, but decided to give it to him because I did not want to have such a large amount of money with me at the hairdresser. I walked home from the hairdresser only to find that Teddy had disappeared again. Again, he did not answer his phone when I called. The next evening, I was awakened by a phone call from Teddy. He had stayed the night at a co-worker's home. He had introduced me to this co-worker weeks before. I had even picked up this co-worker to take him to work and bring him back home. His co-worker talked to me and convinced me to forgive Teddy. Teddy always promised, he would never do this again. His sister told me, it was his addiction. I had no knowledge, Teddy was taking drugs. I thought he was involved with someone else. The next time he disappeared for several days, I decided to have his phone service suspended. He could not make or receive calls. He came home. He was angry. We argued. I was very uncomfortable and had no idea what he would do, so I left the apartment screaming. My neighbors heard me and called the police. Teddy was arrested. I felt relieved. I went to court the next day. When Teddy saw me he cried like a baby. He stated, "You do love me." He kept saying, "I am so sorry." I told the judge, he had been drinking, and he needed help. I called Teddy's family members, so if they called and did not reach him, they would not worry. His sisters, his brother, his mother and his daughter were all very supportive of me and very polite. Teddy decided to stay in jail because he was arrested weeks before for driving without a license. His license was suspended because he was behind in his child support payments. He served 90 days in jail. I was there for every visiting hour and supported him financially. We wrote letters, and I saw him twice a week for 15 minutes. He was transported to another facility because it was crowded in Athens. I drove about 40 minutes once a week to the other facility to visit him. Visiting day was Sunday for 20 minutes. I did not go to church those Sundays because the visiting time conflicted with the time church was in session. I did, however, go to Bible study on Wednesday nights.

Teddy and I continued writing and talking on the phone. Each phone call was 15 minutes or less. I had to prepay for the services. Twenty-five dollars was the minimum amount allowed. The cost was approximately five dollars per phone call. Teddy was finally released after 90 days. He was not allowed on the property where we lived, so I moved. The Mercedes Benz would not function anymore, so I flew to Florida to get my new car from my son. I told my son to make certain to get a ride to and from school. There was no transportation from my new place. The day I left to get my car was the day Teddy was to return home. Arrangements were made for someone to pick him up. I was driving home when Teddy arrived home. My daughter was visiting me at the time and was home when Teddy arrived. Teddy made up some story about going to buy her food and asked to use her car. I came home expecting to see Teddy. Teddy never came home. I called him and he did not answer his phone. I felt embarrassed and had no explanation for my daughter. When Teddy returned the next day, my daughter got in her car and left. Teddy made up some story that he had to drive to Columbus because he had to straighten out a situation there that could have landed him in jail. I knew he had a parole officer in Columbus, so I believed him. My daughter later informed me that there were items missing out of her car. She was missing a camera, and some clothes and shoes. Teddy swore he took nothing out of her car. When I got paid, I gave my daughter $400 hoping to repair the damage of the missing items. Several weeks went by. We were living in our new place with no furniture except a twin bed someone had given us. I slept on the bed, while Teddy slept on the blankets and comforter on the floor. I looked on Craigslist for a bed. I found someone selling a queen size bed for $150. Teddy and I went to see the furniture. We agreed to purchase the bed. She also had a sofa we wanted. She sold us the bed and sofa for $200. I gave her $100 and Teddy was to pay her the next day and make arrangements to bring the furniture home. Again, Teddy disappeared. He did not answer his phone when I called. I made arrangements to pick up the furniture and asked a co-worker to help me take it to my home. I decided that I would break off the relationship with Teddy. No relationship was worth the disrespect I was getting. I did look for facilities to give Teddy the option of getting help or getting out of my life. When he finally came home, he said he would tell me the truth. He was snorting cocaine behind my back. He decided he would not do drugs anymore and he would go into a facility to get help. I told him, I am happy he said that because I was going to tell him to get help or get out. He stated he never cheated on me. He was always doing drugs. He said he did not want to leave me, and will never snort cocaine again. He said I am to be in charge of the monies he receives.

I made the decision to forgive him. My daughter did not speak to me for days. I decided to just pray and allow God to work on Teddy. It was Christmas vacation and I was home for two weeks. Teddy said, "I am so glad you are home." It seems he cannot trust himself. We talked and talked and talked. I know our love for one another is real. He treats me like a queen when we are alone. He cooks for me, serve me, and tell me how beautiful I am. He also likes to tease me and make me laugh. He loves to watch movies and want me to watch it with him. He loves sports and sometimes, I watch the game with him. So far, he still craves beer and cigarettes. I am looking forward to the day when Teddy stops drinking and smoking. Teddy has a pulmonary disease. Several years ago, he was told by his doctor he would not live long. Every time Teddy lights up a cigarette, he coughs uncontrollably. Teddy has an artistic flair. He writes beautifully and decorates the apartment. He said, he went to college to become an interior decorator, but dropped out of school to sell drugs. He also cooks very well. His fried chicken is delicious. I am praying for our relationship to succeed and for Teddy's relationship with God to grow.

Jail Again

Teddy decided he wanted to watch the game with a friend of his he had introduced me to. I had to go to work the next morning, so I agreed and told him, I needed the car the next morning. Teddy did not come home all night. The next morning, I called and left a message on his voicemail. I told him if he did not come home with the car, I would call the police. He came home. Later that evening, Teddy was still angry with me. He was angry because, I had his phone line suspended. He asked to use my phone. When he finished making his call, he threw my phone on the floor and broke it. He then, came after me and grabbed my throat. I managed to unlock the door and run outside to my next door neighbors. They took a while before deciding to open their door to let me in. They called the police and Teddy was arrested again. I did not bother to see about Teddy for a week. I then, decided to go to the jail to see about him. He looked pathetic and unkempt. He told me had I not come to see about him, he was planning to go to Florida to look for me and to ask my forgiveness for all he has done to me. I have a home in Florida. Teddy went with me to Florida to see my home and meet my children earlier in our relationship. I bonded Teddy out of jail and he decided he would not ever do drugs again.

Teddy wanted to cook breakfast this particular morning and needed to buy a few items to do so. We needed pancake mix, bacon and eggs. Teddy was already up and ready to go to the store. Teddy has a suspended license due to being behind in his child support payments. I told Teddy, I would drive. I showered and dressed hurriedly to not keep Teddy waiting. I was dressed and needed to fix my hair. Teddy insisted on going alone. I gave in and allowed him to drive alone. He called me to let me know, he met someone he knew at the Wal-Mart and was giving him a ride home on the other side of town. He allowed me to speak with the gentleman knowing I may not believe him. I soon received another call that morning, April 2nd 2011. Teddy told me he was being arrested for drunk driving and he let me know where to come to pick up the car. Teddy is an alcoholic. Beer is the first item he reaches for in the morning and the last item before going to bed. He knows it is against the law to drive and drink, but Teddy does what he wants to do. This time Teddy was sentenced to serve six months.

Teddy and I communicated via telephone almost daily, and I visited him three times a week for fifteen minutes per visit. Teddy made trustee after several weeks of being incarcerated. This means, I was able to visit with him face to face for about one and a half hours twice a week. We sat facing each other throughout the visit. It was mandatory that we sit. There were other inmates who were trustees also. We sat in the kitchen area for the visit. Teddy held my hands for the entire visit. We continued visitation for three months. I decided since I lost my job in Athens, that I needed to go to my home in Florida and apply for jobs there. Teddy agreed; so I left and for the next three months we visited via telephone only. When I arrived home, my house looked as if it were vandalized.

Back Home in Florida

I was really happy to be in my home and to see my grown up children again. They all lived in my home. My daughter had taken over my master bedroom, and her brothers each had their own room. Teddy suggested I get a blow-up bed and place it in the remaining bedroom for me to sleep. I did that for several weeks, but was ready to move back in my bedroom. My daughter finally got a job in Polk County as a high school counselor and moved to Kissimmee. I was finally able to get back into my bedroom.

I went to the garage to retrieve something and got so disgusted that I decided to clean it. I began picking up papers strewn all over the garage floor. My last son Joel came into the garage and was angry because many of the papers strewn onto the garage floor had belonged to him. They were papers he had accumulated while in high school several years ago. Joel insisted I stop cleaning up and began to break up the glass on a large picture I used to have hanging on the wall. I called out to my older son, Justin who was home at the time to let him know what I was about to do. Justin and I left the house and drove to the front of the complex. I then called the police to have Joel arrested before he broke anything else. I then called Joel's dad my former husband, and asked if Joel could live with him and his new wife and family. He agreed. Then, I posted bail for Joel to come out of jail. If his dad had said, no, Joel would have been left in jail.

Teddy and I continued our communication. Teddy told me to leave everything and he would cleanup. It would give him something to do. Weeks passed by, and I did not get hired. Teddy was due out of jail the first week in October, so I went to Columbus, Georgia to pick him up. I stayed with his sister and her husband. When I picked Teddy up, we went back to his sister's house. She had a new home and this was Teddy's first time seeing it. Her mother was home. I showed Teddy around the house and thought we would wait for his sister and her husband to come home from work. Teddy refused to wait to see his sister. We then drove to Athens.

The next day we went to church to say good-bye to the folks we had met and had come to know. We packed everything hired a tuck and moved to Florida. Teddy went to church with me; he met several of our neighbors and was beginning to learn his way around. We never really lived together long because Teddy was always in and out of jail. We had several misunderstandings. Teddy would get angry and pursue other relationships. This went on for some time. I would find another woman's number in his phone listed under his name. I finally was hired to teach mathematics at a high school in Lake County in the first of the year 2012. While I went to work, Teddy was home. He collected disability, so he did not want to get a job or else his disability would be stopped. Months passed by, and I received a phone call from my sister stating she and her family wanted to come for a visit. She also paid my brother's way to Florida, so they could come together. They came in October 2011; my sister her two adult children her male companion, and my brother. My sister was a widow for several years now. My brother and Teddy did not hit it off. Teddy medicated himself with beer. We wanted to have a barbeque, but both Teddy and my brother Dwight decided for himself to be the chef. The food was purchased and Teddy lit the barbeque to grill the chicken and pork chops. Dwight decided to cook the macaroni and cheese. Dwight did not begin fast enough for Teddy. Teddy put the macaroni on to boil and it got soggy. Dwight insisted on going to the store where we bought more macaroni. Dwight complained about Teddy's barbeque because several of the meats were burnt. We salvaged what we could and ate. The next day was Sunday, we all went to church. Teddy always goes to the altar. He asked Dwight to pray with him. Dwight was rather surprised but prayed with him anyway. The next day, Teddy and I had an argument concerning a car I had originally bought for my older son, Justin. Teddy suggested I purchase the car, but that was a mistake. The car was in dire need of repair. The repair took so long that my son purchased his own car after several months. Now the car I had repaired was available. Teddy wanted the car in his name. I of course did not agree. My brother overheard us arguing. I left Teddy in the garage and Dwight went out to the garage, I thought, to talk to Teddy. I soon came back to the garage to witness my brother beating Teddy in the face with his fist. Teddy was sitting on the couch and his arms were blocked by my brother. Teddy could do nothing but receive the punches. My son Justin had just left the house. I was home alone with Teddy and my brother. I yelled at my brother to stop, but he wouldn't. My neighbor heard the screaming and called the police. My brother had stopped beating on Teddy. Teddy got up to run and my brother followed him with a stick. I could not believe what I was seeing. The day before, my brother spent the afternoon with my best friend, Arnette. I was certain Arnette told him things I told her. I chose not to tell my family the bad things that occurred in my relationship with Teddy because I did not want them to hate him. I do believe that someone ought to know the truth of what happens in an individual's relationship, so I would not end up like Stacey Peterson being murdered by her husband and all her family members believing her husband loved her and not suspecting he was the murderer. I had no idea Arnette would tell my brother the things Teddy did to me. Teddy punched me in my eye, he took my vehicle and left me stranded, he caused the dent in the side of my car. Teddy chose not to press charges when the police came. I took Teddy to a hotel nearby and made arrangements for my brother to go home. I had to pay to spend two nights in the hotel and my brother's airfare to return home. It took a while but Teddy's friends finally convinced him, I did not set him up to be beaten by my brother.

It was August and I still did not have a job. My daughter told me to apply to Polk County. I did not apply before because it was too far, so I thought to travel to work. I applied for a mathematics position at several schools and decided whatever God determines will be. The following Sunday, Teddy and I went to church. Teddy decided even though his face was all puffed up, he would still go to church. Of course I had to answer everyone's question concerning what happened. That Sunday, my pastor requested a faith offering. I believed God for a job and decided to give $25 as my faith offering. I got a call from Ridge Community Senior High School the next day and was hired on the spot. The school is about 50 miles from my home. I gave God the praise and began working. Teddy of course was home and every time I came home, Teddy took off with my car. I finally entered my prayer closet and told God, if Teddy will not live for him and be a good husband for me then take him. I chose to be at peace. One evening as I sat in my bed going over the work I was preparing for my students the next day, Teddy entered my room and said, I love you more than any woman black or white. I said nothing. He no longer went out. He cleaned the house, prepared my meals and made my bed. I had to attend a six-week in-service. My daughter also attended this in-service, so once a week I spent the night with her since the in-service ended so late. The last night I spent with my daughter, I came home the next day to find Teddy on the floor of his bedroom. The days prior to this, he used to say to me, "What are you going to do when I'm gone?" I never responded. He folded all the sheets and towels in my linen closet. He put my clothes and shoes in order in my closet.

He put a CD player on a table near my bed with three CDs in them and showed me how to use it. He told me to keep my closets in order, the way he .fixed them. The last day of my in-service, I came home and met Teddy on the floor of his bedroom. My son, Justin was in the next bedroom, sleeping. When I could not get Teddy up, I screamed for Justin. There was a pool of thick blood right above Teddy's head. He had urinated on himself. I wanted Justin to help me give him a bath, but then was afraid he would drown in the tub. I then called for an ambulance. The neighbors came by and I told them what happened. My son, Justin followed me in my car to the hospital. I rode with the ambulance. They took Teddy, and Justin and I sat for hours waiting to see him. I decided to go home to clean up the mess. I cleaned the pool of blood and had to wipe my bed down with bleach because the ambulance workers laid Teddy on my bed. It was about 11:00 p.m. at night. Justin stopped along the road to get a burger on the way back to the hospital. Teddy was in the intensive care unit (ICU). Only blood relatives and spouses are allowed to visit their loved ones when they are placed in ICU. Teddy and I were not married, but for some reason, the nurse allowed me to see him. I called his sister Cheryl, the minister to let her speak to him. Teddy told me to tell her he loved her. He said to her he was okay. Believing Teddy was about to die, she asked me to pray the sinner's prayer with him. I did and Teddy responded positively. I then said goodbye to Cheryl on the phone. He then took off his mask that provided air, and told me to kiss him. I put my lips to his. He then told me he loved me and gave me a long stare. I said nothing. I looked at his eyes and they were yellow. I told him I would see him in the morning not realizing, I would never see him again. I got a phone call about 1:00 a.m. October 11, 2012 stating that he took a turn for the worse. I told them to please call me when he passes. I called Cheryl to let her know he took a turn for the worse. They called me back an hour later to let me know he didn't make it. I began sobbing. It was unreal; Teddy was gone. God had reminded me of my prayer.

I did feel a sense of relief. I went through his things and found the pictures of the girls he referred to when he said to me I love you more than any girl black or white. He had a picture of a black girl sitting on my car smiling. He had another picture of a white girl. I showed them to my son Justin and then tore them up and threw them away. I was very angry, but chose to say nothing to anyone but Justin. My best friend Arnette called me when she heard that Teddy passed. We had not spoken for months since the beating incidence. She said to me, "You sound angry." She always knows what is going on with me even though I haven't told her anything. I chose to keep the reason I was angry to myself for the time being.

Teddy's sisters and brother-in-law came to Florida for the memorial service. I used a picture Teddy had taken when my sister visited a few months earlier, with Teddy in a suit standing in front of the house. Teddy always said he did not want anyone staring down at him, so I had him cremated. Since Teddy's divorce had not gone through, he was legally still married to Louise. His friend in Michigan told me Louise is receiving his money so I was not to pay for anything. Louise was very kind to me on the phone. She paid for the cremation and I sent the ashes to his daughter.

A New Relationship or a Big Mistake

Teddy and I had made plans to go to Detroit Michigan to see his biological mother. She was diagnosed with cancer and had not seen her son in years and wanted to see him. I put together the trip after speaking with her. Teddy died two weeks before we plan to leave. The day before we planned to leave, his cousin called. I told him Teddy was no longer with us. He obviously was stunned. He replied, "What did you say?" I told him Teddy passed away. He started to cry. I told him we could talk later after he composed himself. We spoke briefly about his cousin's illness and death. I asked him if he was married. He said, "No who would want to marry me?" We continued talking; he wanted me to send him pictures of Teddy and me. Several days later, he wrote me via text to remind me to send him the pictures. He then asked me via text if I had a picture of myself in my phone. I did, and sent it to him. He told me I looked good. When then began talking on a daily basis. I was angry with Teddy and I believe unconsciously I would get back at him by dating his cousin. It was his cousin's idea to keep our relationship a secret. He said one of Teddy's sisters would definitely not like the idea of our seeing one another. He said he was out of work for more than a year. I wanted to meet him in person because the picture he sent me was not close enough for me to see his face. He said all the right things on the phone. He was two years younger than I. I thought I met a man who wanted to turn his life around and wanted the same things I did, friendship, travel partner and respect. I helped him to come here where I live in Florida. He was supposed to spend some time and then return to California. Well, he never returned. I allowed him to stay in the bedroom Teddy used to stay in. My younger son helped him to get a job as a dishwasher at a nearby restaurant. I need to mention when I picked him up from the airport, I was disappointed. He was not as attractive as I anticipated, but I decided to make the best of things. He was helpful in getting Teddy's clothes packed and delivered to a nearby Teen Challenge. He met all of my children, and they liked him. He worked from afternoon to evenings. I allowed him to use my car as transport. He quickly found a drug dealer to sell him weed. He came home smelling awful and told me he was high. He did tell me he smoked weed, but I thought it was in his past. He was very strange. I took him to church and told him this was my life. He was raised a Jehovah's Witness and did not want to live a Christian life. One night he desired sexual favors and treated me like a whore. He said things to me I could not believe. I felt like trash. I had to come to this place to realize like the prodigal son, I am a child of God. My Father owns everything. I should not be living like this. I did not want to put this cousin out in the street. I felt responsible for him being here, so I called the homeless shelter not far away and they had room. I felt delivered. I told him I would take him to the homeless shelter. He did not want to go, so I called the police. I told the policeman I made a mistake by having this individual in my home, and I no longer wanted him here. I told him I called the shelter and they had a place for him. The policeman was familiar with the shelter and offered to take him for me.

He said, Now are you sure they have room?" I said yes and Teddy's cousin had to go. He wanted to rectify the relationship. I was kind enough to do his laundry and feed him. I decided I no longer wanted him in my home. I told him where the Laundromat was. He asked me where he could get the detergent. I named several stores including the local Wal-mart. He was able to find a way to work and do his own laundry. I had not heard from him in weeks; I was happy. He still had some of his clothes in my house because the shelter could not house all his things. I got a phone call from him telling me he was thrown out of the shelter and he wanted his suitcases to pack his clothes. I told him I would bring the suitcases, but he could not come back here to my home. I did not even want to see him. I drove to the shelter with the suitcases; I saw the manager. I asked him what happened. He told me he could not discuss that with me. I told him we were in a relationship, but he acted crazy. The manager replied, "He acted crazy here too." He told me I could leave the suitcases with him and text the guy if I did not want to see him. I did as he suggested. As I drove down the street, I saw him, but kept on driving. I texted him to let him know I left his suitcases at the shelter. I suppose he got the message, I no longer want him in my life. I received a phone call from him after several weeks. He made certain to call me when I could not take the call. He knew my hours at work. He said something about his pay being taken from him and he wanted to borrow $20 to eat. He had the nerve to say he never asked me for anything. He took money from me and never paid it back. He claimed, Oh I took the money to give it back to you when I get paid this weekend. My Christian upbringing would never allow me to say no, especially if someone needed something to eat, but I have grown. I said, "No". He works in a restaurant, if he needed something to eat, he could tell them his struggles. I told him I have no one to ask for help but Jesus, and he is not my responsibility. I have not heard from him since. Whenever I get mail belonging to him, I drop it off at the restaurant. Sometimes, they will tell me he is there, but I say it is not necessary for me to see him.

Both Teddy and his cousin were "Bad Boys". I learned this watching Steve Harvey the other night. He had a young lady on his show who said she was attracted to "Bad Boys". She shared her text messages from her Bad Boy boyfriend, which showed how he had absolutely no respect for her. I am so happy Steve caused that young lady to see she was worth more than what she was allowing to happen to her. I sure wish I could have seen this episode of Steve's show a couple of years ago. I did however end the relationship with Teddy's cousin very early on. Thank God!

I do want a relationship, but I need to wait for God to send me a Godly man. I am through with men who want a woman to take care of them financially and who have no desire to serve the Lord. If you told me earlier in my life I would allow men in my life to take advantage of me, I would say you are crazy; I would never let that happen. I watched many episodes of court shows on television where the woman is trying to get back the money she gave or loaned her boyfriend or lover. I would be too ashamed to go on one of those shows. I chose to write instead. If my story could help some young woman avoid the pitfalls of life, I have done my job. My brother tells me, I have low self-esteem. I do not agree. I was lonely, But God...

A New Beginning

I have decided to attend a different church. I always wanted to attend this church, but thought the distance was too far. I travel 50 miles to work now. My sister, who is a god-fearing woman said to me, "If you can travel far to go to work, you can travel far to go to church." She is right. I am so happy I made the decision to do so. The first Sunday I attended the Pastor made an altar call. I went up to the front to publicly apologize to God even though I had already done so in my prayer closet at home. I now have renewed my relationship with God. He never left me. I always prayed even though my lifestyle was not pleasing to Him. I was baptized again; there were several hundred people baptized that Sunday morning. It was my privilege to be baptized by the Pastor. My pastor mentioned, "Do your first works over". My desire is to continue growing in God's grace and wait for him to bring to me the man of my dreams. My life is now headed in the right direction. I have apologized to my grown children. Life is still lonely at times, But God…